Original title:
On the Wings of Tomorrow

Author: Daisy Dewi
ISBN HARDBACK: 978-9908-1-4054-4
ISBN PAPERBACK: 978-9908-1-4055-1
ISBN EBOOK: 978-9908-1-4056-8

Reaching Beyond Today

In the dawn's gentle light, we dream,
Hoping for futures, bright as a beam.
With whispers of courage, we take our stand,
Embracing the moments, hand in hand.

Through shadows and doubts, we tread the path,
With hearts full of love, we embrace the math.
Each step a promise, each breath a chance,
To dance with the stars in a timeless trance.

With mountains to climb, and rivers to cross,
We learn from the past, embracing the loss.
For every defeat, a lesson to grow,
In the tapestry of life, with threads we sew.

As seasons will change, and time will flow,
We stand united, together we glow.
In laughter and tears, our spirits will soar,
Reaching beyond, always craving more.

So let us ignite the fire within,
With hearts intertwined, let the journey begin.
For each new tomorrow holds treasure untold,
Reaching beyond today, brave and bold.

Soaring Beyond Shadows

In the silence, fears take flight,
Wings unfurl, chasing the light.
Whispers of courage, soft and low,
Lift the heart, let the spirit flow.

Beneath the weight, we rise anew,
Casting off chains, breaking through.
With each heartbeat, we embrace the sky,
Soaring forth, reaching high.

Echoes of dreams in the cool, crisp air,
Daring to chase what once seemed rare.
The horizon beckons with its warm golden hue,
Inviting the bold, the brave, the few.

Through clouds of doubt and shadows cast,
With hope as our guide, we rise at last.
Unfurl the banner of desires inside,
Soar beyond every doubt, every tide.

Awake, arise as the dawn breaks free,
Discovering realms where we long to be.
For in the flight, we find our song,
Soaring beyond, where dreams belong.

New Beginnings in Flight

With the dawn, the world awakes,
New paths unfurl with every step it takes.
In the chill of morning, hope ignites,
Promising journeys, new delights.

Leaping forward, hearts made bold,
Stories waiting, yet untold.
Each moment counts, a canvas bright,
Painting dreams in purest light.

Wings of change begin to spread,
Carrying whispers of what's ahead.
Embrace the winds, let go of the past,
For in this moment, freedom's cast.

Above the clouds, the vision clears,
Casting away shadows, letting go of fears.
With every heartbeat, feel the rise,
New beginnings calling, reach for the skies.

In every heartbeat, a promise rings,
Life unfolds with the joy it brings.
As we soar, our spirits ignite,
In our ascent, new beginnings in flight.

Illuminated Aspirations

Stars ignite in the vast expanse,
Guiding dreams with a radiant dance.
Each shimmer whispers, soft and clear,
Illuminated paths for those who hear.

Through the night, hopes shine bright,
Flickers of courage igniting the sight.
Chasing visions that lead the way,
Illuminated aspirations hold sway.

With every breath, light fills the soul,
Transforming the shadows to make us whole.
In this glow, we find our grace,
A tapestry woven in time and space.

Setting our sights on horizons wide,
With open hearts, we cannot hide.
The light within grows ever strong,
Illuminated aspirations, where we belong.

So let us soar on dreams' soft gleams,
Embrace the challenges, feed the dreams.
For in the light of our shared design,
Aspirations flourish, forever shine.

Following the Call of Tomorrow

A whisper stirs in the still of night,
Calling us gently, pure delight.
With every heartbeat, we feel it near,
Following the call that draws us here.

Through valleys deep and mountains tall,
Echoes of promise in the silence call.
With steadfast passion, we journey on,
Embracing the dawn and the breaking dawn.

In the arms of time, we seek and find,
Paths unfolding, beautifully aligned.
With courage as compass, we navigate,
Following the call, we celebrate.

Through storms and shadows, dreams arise,
Guided by stars in expansive skies.
With every step toward what must be,
Tomorrow's spirit whispers, setting us free.

Hearts aflame, we dance with fate,
In every heartbeat, dreams await.
For in the journey where we roam,
We find our purpose, we find our home.

The Light Beyond the Horizon

In the distance, a glow appears,
Guiding us through our darkest fears.
Colors dance as day breaks free,
A promise of hope for you and me.

Waves of gold lace the silent sea,
Whispers of dreams in the gentle breeze.
With open hearts, we chase the light,
And find our way through the endless night.

The sun rises, painting the sky,
With shades of love that never die.
Every dawn brings a chance reborn,
To seek the joys that life has sworn.

Through valleys deep and mountains high,
The light beckons, a soft, sweet sigh.
Together we'll walk, hand in hand,
Towards the glow of a promised land.

So let us journey, brave and bold,
Chasing dreams, let the story unfold.
For the light beyond the horizon shines,
As we step forward, our fate aligns.

Rising to New Heights

When the morning breaks with fresh delight,
We stretch our wings, prepared for flight.
Every challenge, a chance to grow,
To reach the peaks we hardly know.

With every leap, a new path flares,
Guided by hope and tender cares.
We conquer fears, let our spirits soar,
In pursuit of dreams, we yearn for more.

The summit calls, both near and far,
A glimmering chance, our guiding star.
We rise as one, in strength combined,
Leaving the shadows of doubt behind.

Through every storm, we'll stand our ground,
With hearts like eagles, fierce and proud.
Together we strive for the skies above,
Fueled by passion, faith, and love.

So let us climb where the eagles roam,
Carving our paths, finding our home.
In the heights we dream, we'll find our way,
Rising to new heights, day by day.

The Serendipity of Flight

A sudden breeze, an open door,
Leading us to worlds we adore.
With every beat of our eager wings,
We dance with fate; oh, what joy it brings.

Above the clouds, where dreams ignite,
The air is filled with pure delight.
With hearts unchained, we glide and weave,
In this grand tale, we dare to believe.

Moments unexpected guide our way,
Through valleys lush and skies of gray.
In every twist, a treasure waits,
Hidden in life's delightful fates.

The world below, a tapestry bright,
In colors that burst in the glowing light.
With each ascent, our spirits climb,
Touching the echoes of peace and time.

So let us soar, as the sun dips low,
In this serendipity, we'll find our flow.
For in each flight, we weave our fate,
Writing stories that time won't wait.

Dreams in the Making

In the quiet hours, we dare to dream,
Woven in hopes, a radiant seam.
Every thought a stepping stone,
Creating paths where love is sown.

With eyes alight, we chase the stars,
Transcending limits, overcoming scars.
In whispered wishes, our hearts awake,
Crafting futures, our dreams to stake.

With every heartbeat, visions grow,
Painting the canvas we long to know.
The journey starts with a single spark,
Illuminating the paths through dark.

As dawn breaks softly on our plans,
We lift our spirits with tender hands.
In the embrace of a new-found chance,
We find our rhythm, our sacred dance.

So let us nurture the seeds we've sown,
In the garden of dreams where love is grown.
For dreams in the making are worth the wait,
Bringing to life our cherished fate.

The Skies of What Could Be

In the dawn where dreams reside,
Wings unfold, hearts open wide.
Clouds whisper tales on golden rays,
Each moment shines, in endless ways.

Thoughts drift high on gentle breeze,
Chasing hopes through the swaying trees.
Stars beckon forth, a silken thread,
To weave the paths where dreams have led.

Past the shadows, where doubts convene,
A vision bright, forever seen.
Colors merge in twilight's glow,
Painting futures we yearn to know.

Voices echo in twilight's grace,
Mapping journeys in endless space.
Every heartbeat, a step anew,
Towards horizons where skies are blue.

The skies beckon with tales untold,
In whispers soft, the brave and bold.
With hope as guide, we'll find the way,
In the skies of what could be today.

Journey into the Unseen

Through the mist where silence dwells,
Secrets hide in whispered spells.
Footsteps lead to the unknown,
Where dreams awaken, seeds are sown.

In shadows deep, the light will burst,
Seeding truths within the thirst.
Eyes wide open, heart in tune,
Guided by the silver moon.

Voices calling from afar,
Mapping paths guided by a star.
Across the canvas of the night,
We seek the spark, the inner light.

Each step forward, a tale unfolds,
In the absence of what we hold.
Brave the dark, for dawn will glow,
A journey into the unseen flow.

With each embrace of change we find,
New horizons etched in mind.
The unseen world reveals its grace,
A journey leads us to our place.

Luminous Aspirations

In the depths of a starless night,
Dreams ignite with a gentle light.
Whispers of hope dance in the air,
Painting moments with colors rare.

Aspirations rise like morning dew,
Each drop reflecting a vision true.
Hearts aflame with passions bright,
Guided forth by the inner light.

Boundless skies call out our name,
Chasing visions, fanning the flame.
Every heartbeat, a step we take,
In luminous paths, our souls awake.

Clouds may gather, storms may roar,
Yet we stand firm on the shore.
Through the tempest, we find our way,
With luminous dreams that won’t delay.

Through horizons vast, we'll soar and glide,
With visions bold, forever our guide.
In the tapestry of night and day,
Luminous aspirations, here to stay.

Songs of the Tomorrow Winds

In the whispers of the flowing streams,
Tomorrow sings its hopeful dreams.
Melodies carried on the breeze,
Echo through the swaying trees.

Each note dances, a gentle flight,
Guiding hearts toward the light.
With every gust, a promise made,
In songs of tomorrow, fear will fade.

Voices soft as the twilight's kiss,
Binding spirits in tranquil bliss.
Harmonies weave through the air,
In glorious visions, we share the care.

The future calls in rhythmic tune,
A symphony beneath the moon.
With every breath, let hope expand,
In songs of tomorrow, hand in hand.

Each whisper, a story yet to write,
Carried forth by the winds of light.
In unity, our spirits blend,
In songs of the tomorrow winds, we mend.

Tomorrow's Breath

In the dawn's gentle light,
New dreams take their flight,
Whispers of hope arise,
Under wide open skies.

Chasing the stars above,
With courage and love,
The heart leads the way,
Into a bright new day.

Every step we dare take,
On paths we will make,
Is filled with a spark,
That lights up the dark.

Together we'll run fast,
Leaving shadows cast,
Embracing the chance,
To join in a dance.

With each breath we claim,
Nothing feels the same,
Tomorrow's our song,
In the world we belong.

A Future Beckons

A future shines bright,
Like stars in the night,
Calling us to explore,
And dream even more.

Through valleys and peaks,
The adventure speaks,
With every mile traced,
New wonders we're faced.

In the warmth of the sun,
Our journey's begun,
With laughter and tears,
We conquer our fears.

Paths winding and free,
Invite you and me,
To soar high above,
With passion and love.

So take my hand tight,
As we chase the light,
The future we're given,
Together we're living.

Soaring Through Time

With wings made of dreams,
We travel in streams,
To places unknown,
Where wild hearts have grown.

In moments we blend,
As beginnings extend,
Time dances with grace,
In this timeless space.

Every heartbeat a thrill,
Bringing forth new will,
With a whispering breeze,
We navigate trees.

Together we'll fly far,
Beyond every star,
In this endless sky,
We learn how to fly.

Soaring, we remain,
Free from all the pain,
In the arms of the night,
We find our own light.

The Call of New Skies

The call of new skies,
Whispers soft as sighs,
Inviting the brave,
To challenge the wave.

Beyond the horizon,
The tales are risin',
With each fleeting glance,
A moment to dance.

Embracing the shift,
In time's gentle lift,
We'll follow the wind,
Where journeys begin.

The clouds sing a song,
Of where we belong,
With echoes of grace,
We'll find our own place.

So come, hear the call,
For it's meant for us all,
To paint our own fate,
Before it's too late.

Where Hope Takes Flight

In the dawn's soft embrace, we rise,
With dreams that glimmer in our eyes.
The weight of doubt begins to fade,
As courage paints the path we've made.

Above the clouds, our spirits soar,
Each heartbeat whispers, 'There’s more in store.'
We chase the winds, unbound and free,
Where hope finds wings, and we believe.

Through trials faced and lessons learned,
In every twist, a flame still burned.
With every step, we gain our might,
Together, we will seek the light.

The sky unfolds, a canvas vast,
Each moment more than just a past.
With hearts aligned, we’ll write our song,
A symphony where we belong.

So let us dare to reach for stars,
To bridge the worlds, erase the bars.
For in our hearts, the truth ignites,
Where hope takes flight on endless nights.

A New Chapter in the Air

A whisper calls from distant skies,
A chance to grow, a sweet surprise.
With every breath, a story new,
Unfolding paths where dreams break through.

The winds of change begin to blow,
With open hearts, we chance to go.
In uncharted realms, we'll find our way,
As dawn brings forth a brand-new day.

With joy we turn the page at last,
Embracing futures, leaving past.
The ink dries slow, but words take flight,
In every color, bold and bright.

We gather hope, like scattered seeds,
Each thought a beacon, meeting needs.
Together, stronger, we embrace,
A shining tale, a shared embrace.

So let us write this grand design,
With every heart, with every line.
As we ascend, we'll boldly dare,
To live this life, a chapter rare.

Glimmers of Tomorrow's Light

In shadows deep, a flicker glows,
As dawn approaches, hope bestows.
The path ahead may twist and bend,
But glimmers shine around the end.

With every step, we find our way,
Through whispered doubts and fears that sway.
The light descends, a gentle guide,
Illuminating dreams inside.

A tapestry of time we weave,
In colors bright, we won't deceive.
Each thread a chance, a moment clear,
To shape the future, hold it dear.

In hearts united, strength ignites,
Banishing the darkest nights.
With every breath, we rise, unite,
For in our core, the sparks are bright.

So let the glimmers lead us on,
To chase the dawn, to greet the dawn.
Together, in this radiant flight,
We'll discover all tomorrow's light.

A Horizon Unfolds

Beyond the mountains, wide and free,
A horizon calls, inviting me.
With every sunrise, dreams expand,
A journey starts with steps we planned.

The colors merge in soft embrace,
Painting futures we will face.
With open hearts and minds so bright,
Together, we will chase the light.

Clouds may linger, storms may brew,
But hope persists in skies so blue.
We'll sail beyond the fears we hold,
A brave new world, a tale retold.

In every corner, paths align,
The stars above, our hearts combine.
With gratitude, our spirits soar,
Unfolding magic, forevermore.

So fear not change, nor let it bind,
For in the journey, peace we find.
As dawn awakes, our spirits bold,
A horizon waits, a tale unfolds.

Lifting Shadows of Yesterday

In the dawn's gentle light,
We shed weights of the night.
Whispers of hope arise,
Beneath vast, open skies.

Memories softly fade,
In the warmth, unafraid.
Chasing the morning sun,
New journeys have begun.

Each step a brand new page,
Breaking free from the cage.
Dreams rekindled with grace,
In time's ever-flowing race.

The past is but a tale,
As we chart our own trail.
With courage in our hearts,
A fresh story imparts.

So let the shadows go,
As the bright futures glow.
In unity we rise,
With hope that never dies.

A Future in Flight

Wings spread wide in the breeze,
Soaring high with such ease.
Above the clouds we roam,
In this sky, we find home.

Dreams like feathers we chase,
In a timeless embrace.
Each moment, pure delight,
In a future so bright.

With the stars as our guide,
In this journey, we ride.
Every heartbeat aligns,
In the rhythm of signs.

Hope whispers through the night,
As we dance with the light.
A symphony in the air,
With visions we can share.

Rising up like the dawn,
In this life, we lean on.
Together, we will thrive,
In the dreams we contrive.

Dreams of a New Day

Awake to the soft glow,
Where the wildflowers grow.
Each petal tells a story,
In the morning's glory.

With the sun's warm embrace,
We find our rightful place.
Hopes painted in hues bright,
Ignite the day with light.

Every step a fresh beat,
As the world feels complete.
In the laughter of friends,
A new journey transcends.

Through valleys and the hills,
Chasing the heart that thrills.
In the dance of today,
We find our own true way.

With dreams that intertwine,
In the day’s grand design.
Together we will rise,
To touch the endless skies.

The Promise of New Heights

Climbing mountains unseen,
With a spirit so keen.
Each challenge holds a key,
Unlocking who we'll be.

In the mist, we will find,
The strength of heart and mind.
Winds of change gently guide,
As we reach for the skies.

Every summit we scale,
Tells of courage and tale.
With each heartbeat steep,
There are dreams still to keep.

Together, hand in hand,
We will conquer the land.
With hope as our delight,
We will soar, day and night.

In the journey we share,
With love beyond compare.
The heights we will claim,
In this beautiful game.

The Prophecy of Flight

In the dawn's soft glow, they rise,
Wings spread wide beneath the skies.
Whispers of dreams, they chase the breeze,
In every heartbeat, the spirit frees.

Casting shadows on the ground,
In silence, their truth is found.
A journey begins with every beat,
A symphony played in the heart's seat.

Through valleys low and mountains high,
They soar where eagles dare to fly.
Each feather tells a tale untold,
Of visions bright and destinies bold.

With every flutter, a soul ignites,
Carved in starlight, they touch new heights.
The prophecy waits as they ascend,
Boundless horizons, where time will bend.

So let them rise, let them pursue,
The skies await, vast and blue.
For in their flight lies a truth so grand,
In every heartbeat, a wonder planned.

Ephemeral Echoes of Future Days

Fleeting moments swirl like dust,
Whispers of time wrapped in trust.
In shadows cast by the setting sun,
The echoes dance, a race begun.

Through walls of time, they slip and glide,
In gentle tugs of the rising tide.
Each murmur calls from days ahead,
A tapestry of dreams unfed.

The footprints left in softest light,
Can vanish swiftly, lost from sight.
Yet still they linger, softly call,
In the heart's chamber, they enthrall.

With every pause, the present weaves,
A fabric rich in hopes and leaves.
Tomorrow's wishes, softly play,
As ephemeral echoes shape the day.

So embrace the now, release the fear,
In whispered dreams, the future's near.
For in these echoes, we find our way,
Through fleeting shadows of future days.

Bound for New Frontiers

Across the ocean's wild embrace,
Adventurers seek a timeless place.
With maps unfurled, they chase the dawn,
In every heartbeat, a dream is drawn.

Through valleys deep and mountains steep,
They tread the paths that secrets keep.
A compass spins in the heart's command,
For new frontiers await at hand.

In every step, they cultivate,
The seeds of courage, dreams narrate.
The horizon glimmers, whispers loud,
Among the stars, they'll make their vow.

Unity found in every eye,
With hope as vast as the endless sky.
Together they rise, hand in hand,
A journey bright across the land.

So forge ahead with spirits bright,
For boundless realms await in sight.
In every heartbeat, adventure calls,
To new frontiers, where destiny sprawls.

The Flight of Whispers

In twilight's embrace, whispers soar,
Silent secrets at the core.
Gentle breezes carry the sound,
Of hopes and dreams that know no bound.

They weave through trees with tender grace,
Each murmur finds its hidden place.
Stories shared on the evening tide,
In shadows deep, their hearts confide.

The stars above begin to glow,
With whispered tales of long ago.
In sacred night, they dance and glide,
As every secret starts to bide.

Through silent worlds, they glide and spin,
Woven in dreams where all begin.
The flight of whispers, soft and clear,
An endless journey, drawing near.

So listen close to the night’s soft thrill,
For in the quiet, hearts are still.
The flight of whispers, a song anew,
In every heartbeat, whispers true.

Uncharted Journeys Await

Footsteps echo on the shore,
Maps unwritten, tales in store.
Winds will guide us, strong and free,
Setting sail, just you and me.

Stars above, a guiding light,
Through the darkness, into night.
Every wave brings new surprise,
With each dawn, a chance to rise.

Hearts alight with dreams to chase,
Adventurous paths we'll embrace.
In the unknown, we'll find our way,
Hand in hand, we'll seize the day.

Mountains tall or valleys low,
Every step will help us grow.
Uncharted journeys call our name,
Together we will play the game.

As horizons bend and sway,
Join my side, let's drift away.
With hope as our steadfast guide,
Through every storm, we'll turn the tide.

The Dawn's Gentle Embrace

Whispers of the morning light,
Chasing shadows of the night.
Softly breaking, day unfolds,
In its warmth, a tale retold.

Colors dance across the sky,
As the sleepy world sighs.
Fields awakened, flowers bloom,
Filling hearts with sweet perfume.

Birds in flight sing melodies,
Carried forth on gentle breeze.
Each note, a promise to renew,
In the dawn, the world feels new.

Every heartbeat, every dream,
Rising with the sun's soft gleam.
Let us cherish what we see,
In this moment, you and me.

With the dawn, hope reappears,
Washing away all our fears.
Here we stand, the day awaits,
In the dawn, our love relates.

Embracing What Lies Ahead

With open hearts, we move on,
Through the dusk, into the dawn.
Every step, a brand new chance,
In the light, let courage dance.

Mountains rise and valleys fall,
Every challenge makes us tall.
In the face of doubt and dread,
Together, we will forge ahead.

Hold my hand, let fears subside,
Side by side, we'll face the tide.
In the unknown, love will steer,
Guiding us toward what is clear.

Dreams await beyond the bend,
With each sunrise, we can mend.
Trust the journey, trust the way,
In each moment, here we stay.

Time will teach us, hearts will grow,
Through the laughter, through the woe.
Embracing what lies ahead,
With every word that's left unsaid.

The Promise of the Horizon

As the sun dips low and bright,
Promises glow in fading light.
Whispers of the sea do call,
Painting dreams upon the wall.

Glistening waves stretch far and wide,
Holding secrets deep inside.
All that waits beyond the blue,
Awaits the brave, the bold, the true.

With each step, we chase the skies,
Where the land and ocean lies.
Trust the pull of love's design,
As we walk this path divine.

In the twilight, shadows blend,
Every journey finds a friend.
Radiant stars, our guiding map,
In their glow, we take a nap.

At the edge of night we'll stay,
Listening to what dreams convey.
Join me now, the hour is nigh,
For the promise of the sky.

Soaring into Dawn

The sun breaks through the veil of night,
Awakening dreams with golden light.
Wings spread wide, we touch the sky,
With hearts aglow, we start to fly.

Clouds drift softly, painting the morn,
Each breath a promise, a new day born.
Boundless is the world below,
As hopes arise like rivers flow.

In silence whispers, the winds of change,
Moments fleeting, yet never strange.
Embrace the warmth, let spirits lift,
For in this dawn, we find our gifts.

The horizon calls with a gentle sigh,
Every challenge we choose to defy.
Soaring towards a brighter frame,
In the heart's embrace, we play the game.

Together we rise, no longer confined,
In unity, our spirits aligned.
With every heartbeat, skyward we chase,
Into the dawn, we find our place.

Horizons of Hope

Beneath the canvas of endless blue,
New dreams awaken, bright and true.
Mountains may tremble, rivers may bend,
But in the distance, our paths extend.

Through valleys deep, where shadows dwell,
We carry stories; we dare to tell.
With every step, we break the mold,
In fervent whispers, our truths unfold.

Stars may dim, yet they still glow,
Guiding our hearts to the places we know.
With courage steady, we face the night,
Each dawn brings forth a brand new light.

In the midst of change, our spirits soar,
A boundless journey to explore.
Horizons stretch out, vast and wide,
In every heartbeat, hope will guide.

Together we weave through the fabric of time,
With visions gleaming, forever we climb.
In every moment, let love unfold,
In horizons of hope, our dreams take hold.

Flight of New Beginnings

Awake, arise to the morning's call,
New beginnings wait for one and all.
With every breath, the air feels fresh,
In tender moments, our souls enmesh.

With laughter light and courage bold,
We nurture dreams that long to unfold.
Soaring high on wings of grace,
In every heart, we've carved our space.

The dance of time may twist and bend,
Yet in each turn, a chance to mend.
With open arms, we chase the tide,
In every heartbeat, hope will guide.

The skies ahead are painted bright,
With dreams like stars igniting the night.
In the journey forward, we take our flight,
Toward the dawn, our spirits ignite.

Together we rise, like birds in the air,
In the symphony of life, we share.
Each new beginning, a chance to sing,
In the flight of life, we find our wings.

Embrace the Unseen Skies

Beyond the clouds where dreams reside,
In whispers soft, our hopes collide.
To seek the stars that guide our way,
We find the strength to face the day.

Let go of fears, let courage steer,
In the shadows, love draws near.
With every heartbeat, we transcend,
In unity, our spirits blend.

The winds may howl, the storms may rage,
Yet in the chaos, we turn the page.
To walk a path of endless grace,
With open hearts, we find our place.

In unseen skies, where magic flows,
Our dreams take flight, the spirit grows.
With trust as our compass, we boldly roam,
In embrace of the skies, we find our home.

Together we whisper secrets of light,
In the tapestry woven, our hearts ignite.
With every breath, we set our sights,
On horizons bright, embracing new heights.

Soaring into the Unknown

Above the clouds, our hearts take wing,
Adventures call, and hope will sing.
With every breath, we chase the light,
Together we climb, into the night.

The stars unfold their secret ways,
In silence deep, the spirit stays.
Each whisper winds through cosmic space,
A journey bold, a timeless race.

We leave behind what held us fast,
Embracing dreams, the die is cast.
With wings of courage, we shall dare,
To leap into the dusk's sweet air.

No fear to bind, no chains remain,
In newfound realms, we'll break the grain.
With every pulse, a tale untold,
We build our future, brave and bold.

So here's to flight, to spirits free,
In twilight's glow, we'll always be.
Soaring high, with hearts ablaze,
We chase the unknown, all our days.

Dreams in Flight

In the quiet hours of the night,
Dreams take shape, and spirits ignite.
With every wish, we lift our gaze,
To worlds unseen, through misty haze.

From fields of gold to skies of blue,
Imagination paints the view.
Each fleeting thought, a vibrant spark,
Guides us onward, through the dark.

Hope's gentle hand leads us along,
In chorus sweet, our hearts belong.
With whispered dreams, we find our way,
To brighter paths, where shadows sway.

Beyond the stars, our futures glow,
In dreams of flight, we come to know.
With honest grace, we claim our share,
Of lifelong journeys, free from care.

So close your eyes, and take the leap,
For in our dreams, the world is steep.
With open hearts, we will unite,
To soar together, dreams in flight.

The Horizon Awaits

Beyond the hills, where skies are wide,
The horizon calls, we cannot hide.
With every step, new lands we find,
Embracing change, our hearts aligned.

The sun breaks forth, a golden glow,
In fields of green, where wild winds blow.
With courage firm, we seek to roam,
In every heart, we carve a home.

The past behind, we look ahead,
With dreams to weave, and paths to tread.
The horizon beckons, clear and bright,
Awaits our journey, into the light.

With hope as fire, and love as guide,
We venture forth, with spirits wide.
In each new dawn, our souls will rise,
To greet the day, beneath vast skies.

So take my hand, let's wander far,
With open hearts, we'll be the stars.
The horizon calls, our purpose true,
Together now, in all we do.

Embracing the Dawn

Awake, my soul, the day is new,
With tender rays, the sun breaks through.
In every moment, hope is born,
As shadows fade, the darkness torn.

The morning air, so fresh and bright,
Invites us forth, to feel the light.
In quiet whispers, dreams arise,
With open hearts, we touch the skies.

Each breath we take, a promise made,
To cherish joy, let fears cascade.
With hands held tight, we stand as one,
Embracing dawn, where love has spun.

As colors blend, the world awakes,
In harmony, the earth partakes.
We dance to rhythms, bold and free,
In the morning's grace, our spirits flee.

So let us rise, with laughter bright,
To greet the dawn and the pure light.
Together, in this sacred space,
We'll find our path, our boundless grace.

The Unfolding Journey

Every step we take is new,
A path of light, a morning dew.
With whispered hopes, we chase the day,
Along the road, we find our way.

The mountains high, the valleys wide,
Through stormy seas, we will not hide.
With courage held, we march ahead,
In every heart, a dream is spread.

The choices made, the lessons learned,
In every flame, our passion burned.
Through winding trails, we seek the truth,
In every glance, we find our youth.

In shadows cast, we find the light,
With open hearts, we face the night.
Together bound, we journey on,
With every breath, we greet the dawn.

In moments fleeting, memories grow,
With every step, new wonders flow.
Embrace the journey, let it soar,
For life’s a gift, forevermore.

Veils of the Future

Behind the mist, the world awaits,
With dreams in hand, we chart our fates.
Veils of time obscure the view,
Yet hope remains, steadfast and true.

In whispered winds, the secrets hide,
A tapestry where visions bide.
With every thread, a story spun,
A dance of fate, where all begun.

The shadows shift, a glimpse may show,
The paths we take, where hearts will go.
In every choice, a spark ignites,
As dawn breaks forth and ends the nights.

Through trials faced, we find our way,
With courage bold, we seize the day.
With love as guide, we cast aside,
The doubts that linger, the fears that bide.

So let the veils of future lift,
To show us all, the greatest gift.
In hearts that dream, the world unfolds,
A promise bright, in tales retold.

Where Dreams Take Flight

In quiet nights, the dreams arise,
With starlit hopes that touch the skies.
On wings of faith, we soar so high,
Where aspirations learn to fly.

Beyond the clouds, the visions wait,
An open door, a golden gate.
With every heart, a story sung,
Of battles fought, and victories won.

In rainbow hues, our spirits gleam,
Awake, alive, we chase the dream.
With every challenge, strength we find,
A path illuminated, hearts entwined.

Through valleys deep, we make our way,
On roads less traveled, come what may.
In unity, our voices rise,
A symphony beneath the skies.

So let us dare to chase the night,
In colors bright, where dreams take flight.
Together bound, we'll write the tale,
Of lives well-lived, and hearts set sail.

A Dance with Destiny

Beneath the stars, a rhythm plays,
In shadows cast, where spirits sways.
With every breath, we meet our fate,
In moments shared, we celebrate.

The music calls, a gentle pull,
In every heartbeat, a world so full.
With open arms, we greet the chance,
To join the waltz, to share the dance.

In swirling steps, our paths align,
With grace and joy, our souls entwine.
As destiny's song begins to swell,
In every note, a tale to tell.

With every turn, the future gleams,
In endless possibilities and dreams.
With courage held, we take the lead,
In unity, we plant the seed.

So let us dance with hearts so free,
Embracing all that is to be.
In every move, a spark ignites,
A dance with destiny, through endless nights.

A Journey Through Uncharted Air

Wings unfurl with the dawn's grace,
We soar high into the unknown space.
Clouds whisper secrets in the light,
Charting paths of pure delight.

The horizon beckons, a siren's call,
Each breeze a story, a rise, a fall.
With every heartbeat, we drift and glide,
In the currents where dreams reside.

Stars become beacons in the night,
Guiding our hearts with gentle light.
Through storms and sun, we dance and play,
In this realm where shadows sway.

A tale unfolds beyond the skies,
With each ascent, our spirits rise.
Lost in wonder, our souls entwine,
In a journey so divine.

Together we wander, forever we'll roam,
Finding solace in the vastness, our home.
In uncharted air, we find our song,
In the embrace of freedom, where we belong.

The Dawn's Promise

With the first light, shadows flee,
Hope awakens silently.
Golden rays break the night,
A canvas painted in pure light.

Soft whispers of the morn's embrace,
Dew-kissed petals, nature's grace.
Each heartbeat a vow, a new beginning,
In the day's warmth, a sweet winning.

Birdsong dances on gentle air,
Melodies weaving everywhere.
The world stirs from its dreams so deep,
In dawn's promise, we gently leap.

As sunbeams stretch and shadows blend,
We rise with hope; our spirits mend.
In each moment, possibilities gleam,
Turning life into a vivid dream.

Together we'll face whatever may come,
With steadfast hearts, we'll never succumb.
For in the dawn, we find our way,
In its promise, we boldly sway.

Echoes of the Future

In the silence, whispers resound,
Echoes of dreams yet to be found.
Time unravels, like threads in air,
Visions caught in the moment's stare.

Through tangled paths, we navigate,
With every choice, we create our fate.
Ghosts of tomorrow dance in light,
Leading us into the endless night.

Hope is a lantern, glowing bright,
Illuminating shadows with its might.
In each heartbeat, the future flows,
A river of possibility that forever grows.

We write our stories on the stars,
Healing wounds, embracing scars.
With courage, we step into the fray,
In the echoes, we'll find our way.

The future whispers, soft and clear,
A promise held, forever near.
In every heartbeat, a chance to soar,
In the echoes of life, we'll explore.

Dreams in Full Bloom

In the garden of our minds, we sow,
Seeds of wonder begin to grow.
Petals unfurl in colors bright,
Dreams emerge in the warm sunlight.

With every thought, new worlds arise,
Imagination paints across the skies.
Whispers of hope, soft as spring,
In the heart's chorus, the dreams take wing.

The breeze carries fragrance sweet,
In harmony, our souls will meet.
Through trials and joy, we cultivate,
In life's tapestry, we participate.

Each bloom a story, rich and clear,
With laughter and love, we hold dear.
In this sanctuary, we find release,
In dreams unleashed, we grasp our peace.

Together, we'll nurture this sacred ground,
In every heartbeat, a love profound.
For in this bloom, our spirits thrive,
In the garden of dreams, we come alive.

Unwritten Destinies

In shadows deep, we wander free,
Each choice a thread, our tapestry.
Paths untraveled, roads unknown,
In heartbeats, seeds of fate are sown.

With whispered dreams, we dare to soar,
Embrace the storms, seek distant shores.
Through trials faced, our spirits rise,
With open hearts, we claim the skies.

In every moment, futures blend,
As we chase light, on journeys mend.
With every step, the compass sways,
To weave our tales in myriad ways.

Unwritten pages call our name,
In courage found, we seek the flame.
Together bold, we face the night,
In unity, we find our light.

So lift your gaze, let hope ignite,
For every dawn brings endless flight.
In stories shared, our spirits dance,
Embrace the path; seize every chance.

Navigating New Horizons

Across the dawn, the sun ascends,
With dreams anew, the journey bends.
Each heartbeat echoes, bold and bright,
As we set sail into the light.

With sails unfurled, we greet the day,
Embracing change in every sway.
Through trials met, we learn to grow,
Guided by stars, our spirits glow.

The waves may roar, the winds may shift,
Yet hope remains our greatest gift.
With open hearts, we chart our course,
In unity, we find our source.

New shores await, adventures rife,
We dance along the edge of life.
To navigate through storms and calm,
Together strong, we find our balm.

So raise a cheer, for what's in store,
With every step, we seek for more.
In every heartbeat, find the way,
To shine with hope, come what may.

Beyond Today’s Fences

Beyond today's fences, dreams take flight,
Through whispers soft, we'll seek the light.
With every step, we break the mold,
To find the treasures yet untold.

In fields of wild, where secrets bloom,
We'll chase the stars, dispel the gloom.
With courage bold, we'll wander far,
For in our hearts, we hold the spark.

In laughter shared, the bonds we weave,
Together strong, we will believe.
As shadows fade, new visions rise,
In every challenge, wisdom lies.

So let the winds of change unearth,
The hidden paths, the quiet worth.
For every fence is just a frame,
To guide our souls in love's sweet name.

Beyond today, the world awaits,
With open arms, and welcoming gates.
We'll dance through life, our spirits soar,
In unity, forevermore.

The Horizon's Embrace

As daylight fades, the horizon glows,
In twilight's calm, the journey flows.
With every heartbeat, time stands still,
As we embrace the world, we will.

With colors rich that paint the sky,
We seek the truth that dares to fly.
In every shadow, hope resides,
As we step forth, where love abides.

Through winding paths and open roads,
We carve our dreams, release our loads.
With every sunrise, a chance to rise,
To chase the dreams that light our skies.

Together strong, through thick and thin,
In every loss, we learn to win.
With hands held tight, we face the night,
In the horizon's embrace, we find our light.

So let us soar, on wings of grace,
In the dawn's glow, we find our place.
For in the journey, life unfolds,
The horizon's embrace, a story told.

Fluttering into the Unknown

A whispering breeze calls my name,
Through the shadows, I drift untamed.
Wings of courage, flutter and soar,
Into horizons, forevermore.

With each heartbeat, I take the leap,
In dreams of wonder, my soul will seep.
Unfurling colors, vibrant and bright,
Embracing the mystery of the night.

The stars beckon with hopeful light,
Guiding my path, shimmering and bright.
Fear softly fades with each gentle gust,
In the unknown, I find my trust.

Through fields of silence, I wander wide,
In the tapestry of fate, I abide.
Each moment whispers secrets profound,
In the unknown, my spirit is found.

So here I stand, on edges divine,
With open heart, my soul will align.
Fluttering free, I take the chance,
Into the unknown, I joyfully dance.

Awakened Aspirations

In the morning light, dreams arise,
Whispers of purpose beneath the skies.
Awakened hearts, ready to chase,
With every breath, we find our place.

Glistening hopes, like dew on grass,
Fueling the fire that none can surpass.
Climbing mountains, reaching the peak,
Strength in our voices, none can tweak.

The journey calls with a vibrant song,
In unity we stand, we belong.
Strengthened by each other's embrace,
Together we thrive, in this sacred space.

With passion ignited, we spread our wings,
Embracing the change that the future brings.
Awakened aspirations shining bright,
In the tapestry of dreams, we find light.

As the world awakens from its slumber,
We chase the visions, never to wonder.
For in our hearts, a fire burns clear,
Awakened aspirations, we hold dear.

Paths of Potential

Through the forest of choices, I roam,
Each step I take, I carve my home.
Paths diverge like streams in the wood,
With every turn, I seek the good.

A canvas unfolds beneath my feet,
Each moment a brushstroke, bold and sweet.
In the palette of life, colors entwine,
With courage, I know my path will shine.

Embracing the twists, fierce and fair,
In the maze of dreams, I venture with care.
Sowing the seeds of visions anew,
The potential blooms in shades of blue.

With whispers of doubt, I take a stand,
Trusting my heart and guiding hand.
For every challenge is but a step,
On paths of potential, I won't forget.

Together we wander, hand in hand,
Creating a symphony, perfectly planned.
In each connection, our spirits grow,
On paths of potential, we find our glow.

The Flight of Possibilities

Up in the sky, where dreams take flight,
The wings of freedom elevate our sight.
Soaring high with a heart so bold,
In the winds of change, our stories unfold.

Whispers of hope flutter through the air,
In every heartbeat, we sense the dare.
Taking the leap, with joy in our soul,
Chasing the visions that make us whole.

In the dance of clouds, we find our tune,
Embracing the light of the hopeful moon.
Every moment a chance, every sigh a call,
In the flight of possibilities, we cannot fall.

With laughter and dreams, we lift our gaze,
In the endless sky, we seek the praise.
Together we rise, on currents so high,
Celebrating life, as we touch the sky.

The horizon whispers, “Keep moving on,”
In the flight of possibilities, we are reborn.
A journey of wonder, forever we'll chase,
In the tapestry of time, we find our place.

Threads of a Bright Future

In the loom of life we weave,
Colors bright, dreams to achieve.
Hope is threaded through each day,
As we seek the light on our way.

With hands united, hearts align,
Stitching futures, yours and mine.
Every moment, a strand of grace,
Together we'll find our place.

Through trials faced, we stand so tall,
The strength of many will not fall.
We gather threads of joy and pain,
To craft a world where love will reign.

Across the fabric, stories told,
In vibrant hues like threads of gold.
With every knot, a journey starts,
Binding the world, entwined hearts.

In this tapestry, we find our role,
The threads connect, and make us whole.
In each bright future, woven tight,
We journey forth, into the light.

The Ascendance of Daybreak

When the dark begins to fade,
And the light is gently laid.
Whispers of the dawn arise,
Painting hope across the skies.

Birds awaken, songs take flight,
Chasing shadows, welcoming light.
Each ray a promise, bold and true,
A brand new day, all fresh and new.

Golden hues and crimson flames,
Dancing softly, calling names.
The world stirs, a soft embrace,
In the dawn, we find our place.

Morning's breath, a soothing balm,
Nature's chorus, sweet and calm.
With every dawn, a chance renewed,
In daybreak's light, we find our food.

The horizon blushes, dreams ignite,
In daybreak's arms, we find our light.
Together we will rise and stand,
Beneath the sun, hand in hand.

A New Tapestry Unraveled

In threads of old, new stories bloom,
Whispers of change, dispelling gloom.
We unravel what once was tight,
To weave anew in vibrant light.

Patterns shift, designs transform,
Through the chaos, we find the norm.
Each color speaks of dreams untold,
In the fabric, a courage bold.

Time creates a wondrous blend,
Past and future, hand in hand.
With each stitch, we redefine,
A tapestry, both yours and mine.

In moments lost, we find our way,
We forge the bonds, come what may.
Every knot tells tales of strife,
In this cloth, we weave our life.

So let us gather, dream and spin,
Together crafting from within.
A beauty born of every thread,
A masterpiece, where hopes are fed.

Wings of Change

Flutter softly on the breeze,
Wings of hope through swaying trees.
Every whisper tells a tale,
Of new beginnings, we will sail.

In the air, a dance of dreams,
Rising high, life's vibrant streams.
Change is calling, feel its urge,
With every heartbeat, we emerge.

Breaking free from yesterday,
In the light, we find our way.
With wings spread wide, we'll take the flight,
Into the dawn, beyond the night.

Through the storms, we'll brave the skies,
Sailing forth, we shall arise.
Every feather speaks of grace,
In change, we find our sacred space.

So let us soar, and let us glide,
On change's winds, we will ride.
With every beat, our future calls,
Embrace the skies, where freedom falls.

Ascending with the Sunrise

With golden rays, the day begins,
The shadows fade, as light comes in.
A canvas bright, the world anew,
Embracing hope, in every hue.

The birds take flight in joyful song,
The warmth of morning, where we belong.
With every dawn, our spirits rise,
A promise made beneath the skies.

We chase the dreams, from night to day,
With every step, we find our way.
The sun ascends, a blazing fire,
Igniting hearts with true desire.

As colors blend, the moments bloom,
We greet the day, dispelling gloom.
In unified dance, we take our stand,
With faith and courage, hand in hand.

So let us soar with each embrace,
Ascending high, we find our place.
Together bound, we share this flight,
Forever drawn to morning light.

Whispering Future Winds

The winds carry tales, yet untold,
Promising dreams in whispers bold.
They weave through trees, and across the earth,
An echoing call, of hope and worth.

With every breeze, the future speaks,
In gentle tones that softly peak.
Paths unknown, yet hearts aligned,
Guided by whispers, serendipity finds.

We listen close, in quietude,
For signs of change, and fortitude.
These winds of fate, a kinship weave,
In every sigh, we dare believe.

They dance around, with playful grace,
Embracing all, in their warm embrace.
From every corner, lessons grow,
A tapestry rich, a vibrant flow.

So let us trust, in whispered gales,
For they shall guide us through the trails.
With hearts prepared, we'll bravely go,
Into the winds where futures glow.

Seeds of Tomorrow’s Flight

In soil rich, the seeds will lay,
A promise held for a brighter day.
With gentle rains, and sun's warm kiss,
We nurture hopes, in nature's bliss.

Each seed a dream, with roots to bind,
They stretch and yearn, to seek and find.
A journey deep, from earth to sky,
In unity, we learn to fly.

With patience set, they sprout and grow,
Emerging strength in every row.
The winds may sway, the storms may try,
Yet still, they reach, and rise up high.

In bursts of green, the world awakens,
The promise of life, never forsaken.
Each budding leaf, a hope confirmed,
For every seed, a dream discerned.

With open hearts, we plant our share,
In gardens wide, we sow with care.
Tomorrow’s flight, begins today,
As seeds of change, we find our way.

The Skyward Leap

Towards the heavens, we aim to rise,
With silent dreams and hopeful eyes.
In every leap, a chance we take,
A flight to soar, make no mistake.

The clouds we chase, with joy unfurled,
In bounds of faith, we greet the world.
With every heartbeat, daring heights,
A symphony sung in soaring flights.

And in the breeze, our spirits dance,
We seize the moments, take the chance.
For every leap, there's room to grow,
In boldest hues, our dreams will glow.

The stars align, as shadows fade,
With every step, new paths are laid.
We trust the journey, how it's spun,
The skyward leap, we've just begun.

With laughter bright and courage found,
In boundless skies, we gain our ground.
Together we rise, with wings set free,
In this skyward leap, we will be.

A Journey Yet Unwritten

In the silence, whispers call,
New paths waiting to enthrall.
Each step taken, an unknown fate,
Stories waiting to create.

With stars guiding in the night,
Hearts ablaze, fueled by light.
Maps uncharted, hopes set free,
Wandering souls in harmony.

Every moment a new brushstroke,
Life's canvas yet to invoke.
Through valleys low and mountains high,
Dreams ride on the wings of sky.

In the distance, echoes play,
Promises of a bright new day.
With courage as our steadfast guide,
In unity, we shall abide.

The journey holds its mysteries,
In every heart, a tapestry.
With ink of joy and traces of pain,
Every line we draw shall remain.

The Flight of Infinite Possibilities

Above the clouds, where dreams ascend,
A world of wonders round the bend.
Soaring high, the spirit's glee,
In every heart, a chance to be.

The winds of change will lift us high,
Painting colors in the sky.
With every thought, a path is made,
A dance of light that won't soon fade.

Across horizons, visions gleam,
In the distance, we chase the dream.
Ideas bloom like flowers in spring,
Each one gifted, a song to sing.

Infinite journeys, an open door,
Together we shall explore.
With hope as our compass, we ignite,
A future dazzling, bold, and bright.

Hands reaching out, we touch the stars,
With endless dreams, we erase the scars.
In every heartbeat, a choice to fly,
Upon the winds of what might lie.

Rise Above the Darkening Skies

Amidst the clouds, the shadows creep,
Yet in our hearts, the light will seep.
With whispered strength, we brace the storm,
Together, we can transform.

When thunder rolls and echoes loud,
We stand in courage, proud, unbowed.
Through rain and fear, we find our way,
Finding light within the gray.

Each drop that falls, a lesson shared,
In unity, we are prepared.
With arms entwined, we face the night,
In the darkness, we find our light.

The dawn will break, the skies will clear,
In every heart, we hold our cheer.
As rays of hope pierce through the fray,
We rise above, come what may.

So let the storms rage on and roar,
Our spirits strong, forever soar.
In the embrace of each new day,
We find the strength to pave the way.

Horizons Blooming with Potential

Where the earth meets the endless blue,
Horizons whisper of dreams anew.
In every dawn, a canvas wide,
A promise held, a truth inside.

With every step upon the ground,
Hope awakens, softly found.
Fields of passion stretch and grow,
In the heart, the fire flows.

The sun rises on aspirations bright,
Painting the world in colors light.
With dreams as seeds, we sow and tend,
A journey's start, a chance to blend.

Through every storm, in every tear,
We find the strength to persevere.
In the shadows, we plant our seeds,
From quiet moments, greatness leads.

As horizons bloom, we'll chase the sun,
With open hearts, we'll become one.
Embracing every twist and bend,
In the garden of life, we ascend.

Crafted by the Breeze of Change

Whispers of a shifting wind,
Carrying tales of what has been.
New paths carve through ancient stones,
The heart learns to be at home.

Blossoms dance in vibrant air,
Embracing all without a care.
With courage born from softest day,
We rise and greet the dawn's array.

Change draws near, a gentle hand,
Shapes our dreams like shifting sand.
Embrace the flow, the sweet unknown,
In every heart, a seed is sown.

Mountains echo, rivers sigh,
Underneath the sprawling sky.
From every end, a start appears,
Guide us through our hopes and fears.

Within each gust, a story weaves,
Through rustling leaves, our soul believes.
In the dance of night and flame,
We find a spark, we find our name.

Beyond the Eventide

Stars awaken, glitter bright,
Chasing shadows in the night.
Whispers carried by the breeze,
Promises made beneath the trees.

Silhouettes of dreams take flight,
Painting the canvas of delight.
In this moment, hope resides,
As daylight gently slips and hides.

The moon enchants with silver glow,
New paths unfold, we dare to go.
Awake the spirit of the night,
In stillness, we embrace the light.

Time flows softly like a stream,
Guiding us through every dream.
Beyond the dusk, a dawn will rise,
Awakening our wandering eyes.

In this transient world we tread,
Every heartbeat holds a thread.
Beyond the eventide so clear,
We find our way, forever near.

The Map to Uncharted Tomorrows

Ink on paper, paths unfold,
A journey waiting to be told.
With each step, the future bright,
Guided by the stars at night.

Winds of fortune, sailing free,
Charting courses yet to see.
Every wave, a chance to soar,
To lands untouched, to distant shores.

Footprints mark the dreams we chase,
In the vast and open space.
Brave the tides, embrace the dawn,
With every breath, we journey on.

The unknown calls with siren's song,
We gather strength, we grow so strong.
Trust the map within your heart,
For every end, a brand new start.

Through valleys deep, and mountains high,
The spirit learns to spread its sky.
With open hearts, they yearn to go,
To write the tales of tomorrows' glow.

Echoes of Undiscovered Dreams

In the silence where hearts reside,
Dreams awaken and gently guide.
Whispers flourish, truths unfold,
In shadows cast by dreams untold.

A tapestry of thoughts combined,
In every stitch, a spark aligned.
Echoes sing of paths unseen,
Through valleys rare and woodlands green.

Eyes wide open to the night,
Daring souls take courageous flight.
With every breath, we weave the seam,
Embracing echoes of our dream.

Through the stillness, visions flow,
With every heartbeat, visions grow.
Uncharted realms invite our gaze,
To dance upon the mystery's maze.

In the dawn of what could be,
Undiscovered dreams run free.
Let them soar on wings of grace,
In every heart, find your place.

Whispers of the Morning Breeze

Softly sings the morning light,
As dew drops glisten, pure and bright.
Gentle whispers greet the day,
In nature's arms, we long to stay.

Birds take flight, their songs resound,
In emerald fields, dreams are found.
The breeze carries tales anew,
Of hopes awakened, skies so blue.

Each blade of grass, a story spun,
In whispered tones, we become one.
The world unfolds in vibrant hue,
As whispers dance in morning's dew.

A canvas painted, fresh and clear,
With every gust, we cast out fear.
Embrace the warmth, let worries cease,
In morning's breath, we find our peace.

So let us wander hand in hand,
Through fields of gold, a promised land.
With every whisper, every breeze,
We chase the dreams that set us free.

Chasing Sunlit Aspirations

Beneath the dawn, our spirits rise,
A dance of hope beneath blue skies.
We reach for stars, our dreams untold,
In sunlit paths, our hearts unfold.

With every step, we claim our place,
In the bright light, our fears erase.
The horizon calls, a siren's song,
In sync with rhythms, we all belong.

The world ahead, a canvas wide,
With colors bright where dreams abide.
In pursuit of light, we shall not cease,
Our sunlit aspirations bring us peace.

Through valleys deep, on mountain high,
We chase the sun, we learn to fly.
With every heartbeat, every breath,
We forge a path where fears meet death.

Together we rise, united we soar,
Chasing dreams that open every door.
In every dawn, we find our grace,
In the warmth of light, we find our place.

Daring to Leap Beyond

In shadows cast, we find our way,
With courage strong, we face the day.
A leap of faith, a risk to take,
For dreams ignite when we awake.

The edge may tremble, winds may sigh,
Yet in that moment, we learn to fly.
With open hearts, we sail the unknown,
In every leap, new seeds are sown.

The fear of falling, a fleeting thought,
For in each stumble, wisdom's bought.
The vast expanse beckons our name,
In daring leaps, we play the game.

With eyes on horizons, we chase the sun,
Together we rise, our souls as one.
With every jump, we break the chain,
In daring to leap, we feel no pain.

So spread your wings, let courage swell,
For in each leap, we weave our spell.
Beyond the cliffs, beyond the tide,
In daring to leap, our dreams collide.

Navigating Stars of Hope

In the velvet night, dreams arise,
Guided softly by shimmering skies.
Each star a beacon, a distant dream,
In cosmic dance, we find our theme.

Waves of light weave through our hearts,
As hope ignites, the journey starts.
Navigating paths where shadows play,
We chart our course, we find our way.

The whispers of the cosmos call,
In unity, we rise, never fall.
With every twinkle, a wish we send,
In stars of hope, our spirits mend.

Through storms that rage and winds that shift,
In starlit nights, our hearts uplift.
We sail through darkness, hand in hand,
With hope as our compass, together we stand.

So dance beneath the starlit dome,
With every wish, we carve our home.
Navigating life's vast sea,
In stars of hope, we find the key.

Lifting Spirits into Tomorrow

With dawn's first light we rise again,
Hope ignites like a gentle flame.
Casting shadows of yesterday,
We step forth, unburdened by blame.

The horizon whispers of dreams so bright,
In every heartbeat, a song takes flight.
Together we dance on this new road,
Lifting spirits, sharing the load.

With each sunrise, a chance to renew,
To weave the threads of wishes true.
Embrace the path that lies ahead,
For in our hearts, love is widespread.

Through trials faced and storms we've braved,
We'll find the strength to be unshaved.
The future calls with a gentle hand,
And with each step, together we stand.

So lift your gaze to the dawn anew,
Believe in the light that shines for you.
In unity, our spirits will soar,
Into a tomorrow, rich with lore.

Canvas of the Coming Day

A canvas waits, untouched and wide,
Colors blend as dreams collide.
Brush strokes vibrant, bold in hue,
Each moment captured, fresh and true.

With every dawn, we paint our fate,
Creating tales that celebrate.
The sun spills gold upon the scene,
Life unfolds in shades unseen.

From whispers soft to laughter loud,
Each story woven, proud and loud.
On this canvas, we paint our song,
Together, where we all belong.

With every stroke, a memory made,
In hues of joy, no fears invade.
Embracing every shade and tone,
This coming day, we call our own.

And when the night begins to fall,
Our canvas glows, we hear the call.
For in the dark, our dreams ignite,
A testament to our shared light.

When the Stars Align

In the quiet of the midnight sky,
Dreams take wing and spirits fly.
Each star a wish, each shimmer a sign,
A cosmic dance when the stars align.

With hearts aglow, we chase the night,
Finding magic in the soft starlight.
Together we journey, hand in hand,
For in this moment, we understand.

The universe whispers secrets long,
In celestial tides, we rise and belong.
When paths converge, new worlds will find,
The beauty of souls that are intertwined.

In stillness, we hear the gentle call,
A reminder we're never too small.
With every heartbeat, we draw near,
As destiny beckons, crystal clear.

So look to the sky, let your heart soar,
Embrace the dreams waiting in store.
For when the stars grace the moonlit sea,
A tapestry of hope waits for thee.

Boundless Skies Await

Above us stretch the boundless skies,
Endless possibilities, hope that flies.
With every heartbeat, the world expands,
A canvas of dreams crafted by hands.

The winds whisper tales of old and new,
Inviting us forth with skies so blue.
With eyes wide open, we journey far,
Chasing the light of our very own star.

In every sunset, a promise lies,
In shadows softened by twilight sighs.
Embrace the night as it gently falls,
For each dawn breaks with new enthralls.

Together we soar on the wings of fate,
With hearts unburdened, we cultivate.
The dreams that weave through the evening air,
As we dance with hope, unchained and rare.

So raise your gaze to the endless night,
With every step, our spirits take flight.
For boundless skies await us all,
As we gather strength and heed the call.

A Glimpse of What Awaits

In shadows cast, a whisper flows,
Hints of dawn where stillness grows.
Each moment holds a spark of fate,
A promise wrapped in silent weight.

The heart beats soft, the breaking day,
Reveals the paths we dared not stray.
With every step, a choice unfolds,
A story waiting to be told.

Beyond the veil, new worlds arise,
Beneath the tapestry of skies.
The journey's end, a fleeting chance,
Awaits in every dreamer's glance.

A glimpse beyond the veils of time,
Where hopes and shadows softly rhyme.
The future calls, both bright and vast,
Embrace the echoes of the past.

In twilight's hand, the stars align,
A hint of what will soon be mine.
With open arms, I greet the dawn,
For every end, a new life’s drawn.

Chasing the Morning Light

The sun breaks free, the shadows part,
Igniting dreams within the heart.
With every step towards the glow,
New hopes arise, reborn, aglow.

I chase the light that paints the skies,
A canvas bright that never lies.
Each ray I catch, a fleeting chance,
Guiding me through life's wild dance.

The morning whispers soft and clear,
With every breath, I draw it near.
The warmth upon my eager face,
Reminds me of my rightful place.

In open fields, beneath the sun,
I find my peace, my battles won.
The light cascades, it leads the way,
Towards a bright, unfolding day.

With every dawn, a fresh embrace,
Chasing the light, my fears erase.
The journey calls, the path is bright,
As I go on, I chase the light.

Tomorrow’s Canvas

A blank slate waits, so crisp and clear,
With colors bold, it draws me near.
Each stroke a wish, each shade a dream,
In every hue, the hopes redeem.

The brushes dance with vibrant grace,
Creating worlds in open space.
With every line, a story told,
A vision bright, the heart's pure gold.

I paint the dawn with shades of hope,
In every blend, I learn to cope.
The future waits, so rich and wide,
In colors bright, I take my stride.

With every drop, I feel the thrill,
The canvas waits, my dreams to fill.
Tomorrow's light, a daring start,
An open door to paint the heart.

And as the sun sinks low, I sigh,
For art is where the soul can fly.
A tapestry of what I seek,
On tomorrow's canvas, bold and sleek.

Unfurling Dreams

Like petals soft, we start to bloom,
In gentle light, dispelling gloom.
The dreams we hold, like seeds in earth,
Awakening in moments of worth.

With every breath, a story grows,
In whispered winds where passion flows.
The courage found, a spark ignites,
As we embrace the endless heights.

In twilight's hush, the stars align,
Our aspirations intertwine.
With roots held firm, we reach for skies,
Unfurling dreams, our spirits rise.

Through trials faced and doubts expressed,
We find the strength, we feel the fest.
With open hearts, we seek the dawn,
To share the dreams we've woven on.

In every heartbeat, every scheme,
The world ignites around our dream.
Together we can brave the storms,
Unfurling dreams in endless forms.

www.ingramcontent.com/pod-product-compliance
Ingram Content Group UK Ltd.
Pitfield, Milton Keynes, MK11 3LW, UK
UKHW030902221224
452712UK00007B/968

9 789908 140544